EDWARD H. CHAMBERLIN,

by ROMNEY ROBINSON

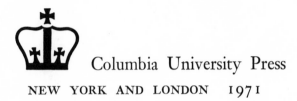

Columbia University Press

NEW YORK AND LONDON   1971

COLUMBIA ESSAYS ON THE GREAT ECONOMISTS
DONALD J. DEWEY, GENERAL EDITOR

Edward H. Chamberlin is Number 1 of the series

INTRODUCTION

AT THE ANNUAL MEETING of the American Economic Association in 1963, a special session was convened to celebrate the thirtieth anniversary of the publication of Edward H. Chamberlin's *The Theory of Monopolistic Competition*. On that occasion, this evaluation of the book was quoted: "the most influential single work ever produced by an American economist." In 1967, the editor of a book of essays compiled in Chamberlin's honor spoke of the "revolutionary impact" of *Monopolistic Competition*, thus echoing the often-expressed view that there have been two revolutions in economic thought in this century—the Keynesian and the Chamberlinian.

The only true revolutions in theory, it has been said, are those which reach into the introductory textbooks. Chamberlin's ideas are by now part and parcel of these texts—but they have been absorbed in a way which conceals the extent of his influence. Any contemporary price theory text will tell its readers that Chamberlinian "monopolistic competition" is one of five possible competitive cases, the others being monopoly, pure or differentiated oligopoly, and pure competition. Often the texts are unenthusiastic about "monopolistic competition." Watson, in his *Price Theory and Its Uses*, says monopolistic competition theory has been "something of a disappointment." Due and Clower say, in *Intermediate Economic Analysis*, that the fields of its possible relevance are limited, and that "study of these fields raises some doubt about the applicability of the assumptions." Leftwich, in *The Price System and Resource Allocation*, says its analysis "is very similar to that of pure competition"; Bilas, in *Microeconomic Theory*, says it is "basically the same as pure competition."

This is hardly the stuff of which revolutions are made. Why then is it said that Chamberlin's work was so influential? What did he contribute to economic thought? We must begin to answer such questions by recognizing that Chamberlin never intended "monopolistic competition" to be simply one of five competitive alternatives. His goal was theory that would cover the *entire spectrum* of real competitive situations, and "monopolistic competition" was always to him a phrase describing the key feature which he saw present in *all* those situations. In fairness to the textbooks, we must note that the narrow case which they call "monopolistic competition" is a case which Chamberlin did explore in considerable detail in his chapters v through vii. But in comparable fairness to Chamberlin, we must note also that in his work subsequent to chapter vii—and virtually all of his professional career was devoted to the pursuit of monopolistic competition theory—he ignored this case almost completely.

We can clarify matters somewhat by looking at two paragraphs from the very opening (pp. 8–9) of *Monopolistic Competition*. Chamberlin has been discussing the two prerequisites for pure competition: a large number of buyers and sellers, and a homogeneous product. He continues:

The two requirements for pure competition suggest at once the two ways in which monopolistic and competitive elements may be blended. In the first place, there may be one, few, or many selling the identical product in the identical market. Here the common market is shared by all, and such control over price as any one has is a control over the single price at which all must sell. A condition of monopoly shades gradually into one of pure competition as the sellers increase in number. The theory of value for the intermediate ground in this case has been treated, mainly by the mathematical economists, with particular reference to the problem of two sellers, or "duopoly," and we may extend this terminology, adding "oligopoly" for a few sellers. . . .

In the second place, sellers may be offering identical, slightly different, or very different products. If they are identical, competition is pure (provided also that the number of sellers is very large). With differentiation appears monopoly, and as it proceeds further, the element of monopoly becomes greater.

Chamberlin simply spells out two significant considerations with respect to the nature of competition: the number of sellers involved and the differentiation or non-differentiation of the product. However run-of-the-mill these ideas may seem today, they were revolutionary in 1933. Earlier discussions of the significance of the number of sellers had been scattered, and they certainly had not been joined to the idea of product differentiation—an idea that was very nearly original with Chamberlin.

In sum, it is largely as a consequence of this single page that the textbooks now tackle matters as they do: they say that analysis of price determination can be broken up into several categories, depending on whether the number of sellers is large or small and the product is differentiated or undifferentiated. Although the whole of *Monopolistic Competition* is devoted to expanding the ideas so expressed, this is the only point in the book at which they are summed up in this manner. It would be difficult to cite any other two paragraphs that have so influenced the course of economic theory.

Chamberlin's ideas met rapid and widespread acceptance partly because of the time of their appearance. They suggested a means of closing a distressingly large gap in price analysis. An elementary theory of monopoly, in something resembling its present form, had existed at least since the appearance of Marshall's *Principles* in 1890. (Actually, Cournot had developed simple monopoly theory much earlier in the 1800s, but his work was largely ignored.) At the other end of the competitive spectrum, the theory of pure (or perfect) competition had been filled out during the 1920s. Thus, elementary theory for the two competitive extremes existed. But where was the theory for competitive situations between these extremes?

Chamberlin's intention was to fill this gap—completely. He began with the idea that almost all actual pricing situations involve a mixture of monopoly and competitive elements. This view was not startlingly original; Chamberlin's innovation was to set out the two concepts by means of which, so he argued, the theory of monopoly could be mixed or blended with the theory of pure competition. They are the concepts indicated in the passage quoted: product differentiation, and oligopoly.

With very few exceptions, Chamberlin said, the product of each single seller is to some degree different from that of his competitors. Even if the products themselves are physically similar or identical, then the seller's location is different, or his personality is. There is always *some* difference—and, of course, in his selling effort each supplier will probably emphasize, if indeed he does not exaggerate, the special qualities which make his product "different." This differentiation, so Chamberlin argued, should be interpreted analytically as a monopoly element: it gives the seller some degree of power to set his own price and establish his own market. And yet, despite this monopoly element, the situation may still be intensely competitive, since in ordinary circumstances other sellers are offering products which are close substitutes for that of the seller in question.

Chamberlin's approach to his second concept, oligopoly, was much less fully developed. In its most elemental form, his reasoning was this: as one proceeds from the case of many sellers to that of few sellers, one is moving toward the single-seller case; hence the theory of few sellers, oligopoly, is close to that of the theory of monopoly. In fact, so Chamberlin said, if numbers are small and each seller recognizes his total influence on market price, the resulting price will be "the monopoly price." But he did not develop this idea at any length—in fact, Chamberlin's oligopoly proposal constitutes one of the most paradoxical incidents in the history of price analysis. It was immediately seized upon, as though economists were by instinct aware of its importance in price determination. Yet the construction of oligopoly analysis has proven exceedingly difficult; to this day, there is nothing even approaching a satisfactory theory of oligopoly situations. To this topic we must return at a later stage.

What is significant for our immediate purposes is that Chamberlin's ideas appeared so promising that they were quickly taken up and translated into the now-conventional fivefold division of competitive situations. Ironically, the detail of this division is almost certainly not what Chamberlin had intended at all (even though, superficially, it may seem in complete harmony with the two paragraphs quoted). This may in part account for the complaints of misinterpretation which appear in his subsequent book, *Towards a More General Theory of Value* (hereafter shortened to *General Theory of Value*). Chamberlin intended monopolistic competition theory to cover all of the gap between the competitive extremes, and even to take in the extremes themselves. This would have meant only two categories: large-group and small-group monopolistic competition. However, events developed otherwise. The new system of classification, which seems to have evolved without formal decision by any individual or group, gave the name "monopolistic competition" to only one of the five categories. It retained monopoly as a separate category, even though Chamberlin is explicit that monopoly ("ordinary monopoly," in his terminology) is simply a particular case within monopolistic competition. It kept also pure (or perfect) competition—the very theory Chamberlin was attacking. Although quite willing to use pure competition as an ingredient in monopolistic competition theory, Chamberlin denied its application in unqualified form to real situations. He conceded a very few cases in which it might be meaningful, but these he wanted to treat as the outer fringe, the extreme limiting case, of large-group monopolistic competition. To endow pure competition with the continuing status of a separate and presumably equal category, adjacent to large-group monopolistic competition, was thus to deny him part of the very objective he had sought.

No doubt these "misinterpretations" arose out of a desire to compromise: to incorporate the new ideas, and yet not part so completely with the old. And by and large, despite some possible measure of distortion, the new *was* incorporated. All of price theory since the publication of *Monopolistic Competition* bears the imprint of Chamberlinian ideas. To understand that theory, with all its dilemmas and deficiencies, we must understand Chamberlin's work.

There are two keys to the interpretation of this work. The first is continuity. At the outset of his career, Chamberlin fastened on the idea that actual pricing situations, almost without exception, involve a mix of monopolistic and competitive elements. He never wavered in his conviction that this was the means by which theory with genuine insight into real pricing situations would be obtained, nor in his belief that product differentiation was the key to the mixture.

The second key is change. It is one thing to be seized of an idea; it is quite another to translate that idea into rigorous, internally consistent theory. Chamberlin's first attempt at theory came in chapters v through vii of *Monopolistic Competition*. As time passed after the book's appearance, and as criticism and comment became available, Chamberlin must have grown increasingly aware of the inadequacies of this attempt. Chapter ix (first added in the fifth edition, in 1946) does not amplify chapters v to vii; instead, it sketches a *different* theory. And in *General Theory of Value*, there is the suggestion of a third and again-different theory.

The textbooks did not follow Chamberlin through these changes; in the main, they have been content to take his first attempt as his final word. So it is not surprising that he should have complained about misinterpretation.

In point of fact, Chamberlin never did succeed in fashioning his basic ideas into satisfactory theory. George Orwell once said that the record of any man's life, viewed from within, is a series of defeats, and this summing-up might well be applied to Chamberlin's life work.

This is not to downgrade Chamberlin's importance. One might say equally of Alfred Marshall, Chamberlin's giant predecessor in the field of price analysis, that he failed, for Marshall was quite unable to work his immense knowledge of actual business practice into a unified theory of price. The shortcomings of Marshall's theoretical structure are sometimes discussed unkindly today—perhaps without sufficient regard for the immensity of the task Marshall had set for himself. Every major figure in economics has ultimately been defeated by the complexity of the problems he has tackled; and part of his conceptual scheme has had to be redone. John Stuart Mill rewrote parts of Adam Smith; and in due time Marshall rewrote considerably more of Mill. Marshall's own work underwent similar revision; and Chamberlin, more than any other single author, is responsible for the differences between today's price texts and Marshall's *Principles*.

Perhaps Chamberlin's basic ideas were wrong. It may be impossible to mix the theories of competition and monopoly in any meaningful sense. Or if the mix *is* possible, the result may contribute little toward a more satisfactory theory of price. In either instance, Chamberlin's standing as a major figure in the record of economic theory remains secure. Although his work was original, it was also a natural consequence of the state of economic thought at the close of the Marshallian period. No attempt at the improvement of price theory is likely to succeed without an understanding of Chamberlin's work, and of the background out of which that work evolved. The purpose of this present study is to contribute to that understanding.

1. MARSHALLIAN ECONOMICS

An essential fact to grasp about Chamberlin's work has already been mentioned: it was a rebellion against orthodox price theory—more specifically, against pure competition theory. The magnitude of this rebellion can be understood only by recalling that in 1933, when *Monopolistic Competition* first appeared, price theory was still absolutely central in economic analysis. The macroeconomic theory of income and employment had not yet emerged.

Chamberlin argued that pure competition theory is significantly and unavoidably *false* as a description of price determination in "the real world." His goal was the construction of different analysis, characterized by accurate description of real conditions.

The comments already cited at the beginning of this study say, in effect, that monopolistic competition is *not* significantly different from pure competition. Although this is a devastating criticism in the light of Chamberlin's objective, it is a valid one, at least with respect to his initial attempt at theory. This attempt drew much too heavily on the very theory Chamberlin wanted to attack. Hence he was forced to try to recast his material in different and less vulnerable terms.

Pure competition theory still has its defenders—and, not surprisingly, they are likely to point out that an attempt to produce something notably different (Chamberlin's initial attempt) yielded something notably similar. Now it is interesting that these defenses of pure competition against monopolistic competition so often appeal to the authority of Alfred Marshall. It is argued that Marshall was the greatest of realists and the most perceptive of economists in matters of actual price determination.

Yet the theory of pure competition is *not* to be found in

Marshall's work. It emerged in the years immediately before and after his death (in 1924), and all that can be said is that by one interpretation, pure competition theory constitutes a logical extension of "what Marshall meant." By another interpretation, Marshall meant nothing of the kind. The plain fact is that it is difficult to establish what he *did* mean. Joseph Schumpeter considered Marshall a landmark figure in economics; yet, in a summing-up he once said of Marshall: "He sensed the intimate organic necessities of economic life even more intensively than he formulated them"—a delicate suggestion that Marshall's "feel" for the quality of economic problems sometimes outran his ability to give clear analytic expression to his insight.

The most common objection to pure competition theory is its assumption that each firm faces a perfectly price-elastic demand curve; that is, it can sell as much as it pleases at a market price over which it has no control. There is no such demand curve in Marshall's work; and his discussion of what he termed "free competition" often sounds very different from the conditions of pure competition.

In this sense, Chamberlin's monopolistic competition theory can fairly be described as an attempt to interpret more fully the world Marshall discussed, even though Chamberlin never claimed to be the bearer of the true Marshallian gospel. In one or two critical respects, Chamberlin departed sharply from Marshallian ideas. In other respects he did not. From 1900 to 1930, Marshall's influence dominated the English-speaking economic world, and Chamberlin remained largely within that tradition. Consequently, if we are to understand either Chamberlin's own ideas or the position he attacked, we must begin by considering Marshall's contribution.

Today's price theory texts are heavily weighted with Marshallian material. (They lack only that mastery of the facts of everyday business experience which was so characteristic of Marshall's work.) Price elasticity of demand, short-run and long-run equilibrium, external and internal economies, marginal utility—these are all Marshallian concepts. But above all, Marshall is associated with a supply-and-demand, *ceteris paribus* approach to the theory of price.

Marshall did not bring "supply and demand" into economics. Instead, he inherited a set of rather nebulous supply-and-demand notions from his classical predecessors, some of whom, in discussing the subject, had committed errors for which an undergraduate student would be penalized today. Marshall refined and clarified these ideas. He drew the now-elementary supply-and-demand diagram (it was Marshall who first introduced the diagrammatic method into economics), and he insisted that both supply curve and demand curve must be drawn on *ceteris paribus* terms—meaning, of course, that if you want to isolate the influence of price on demand (or on supply), you must assume all *other* influencing factors (such as consumer incomes and consumer tastes in the case of demand) constant. He cleared up much of the old dispute about whether supply or demand is more important with respect to price in his unforgettable analogy of a pair of scissors: You cannot claim, he said, that either of the two blades does more of the cutting. (But he added that the supply blade may be slower in making its effects felt.)

Marshall had to begin with his *ceteris paribus* supply-and-demand approach because so many unsettled issues needed to be clarified by this method. He understood, however, that the *ceteris paribus* approach was unrealistic, since in actual experience the "other factors" do not cooperate by remaining unchanged while the consequences of one particular change work themselves out. His objective was a more fully developed theory, properly disciplined by actual experience, with at least part of the *ceteris paribus* scaffolding removed. His classical predecessors had possessed, as Marshall noted, "a wide and direct personal knowledge of business affairs." For some twenty years prior to the publication of his *Principles* in 1890, Marshall set himself to acquiring similar knowledge. It is doubtful that any economist before or since has surpassed Marshall's grasp of the realities of business practice.

The division of competitive situations which Marshall brought from his empirical work, or at any rate which he made in his *Principles*, was simple. There were "open markets" (alternatively, "free competition") and "monopolistic markets." He did not spell out in much detail the properties of either market type, but he did state a basic characteristic of open markets: "only one price in the market at one and the same time." Price uniformity emerges because all market participants have a pretty good idea of what is going on, so that "though everyone acts for himself, his knowledge of what others are doing is supposed to be generally sufficient to prevent him from taking a lower or paying a higher price than others are doing." (*Principles*, pp. 341–42)

Marshall does not seem to have considered monopolistic control over price as a major threat to economic welfare. Any firm which sought to exploit what was technically a monopoly position by charging an exorbitant price could expect, in due course, to be swamped by new competition. Despite a chapter on monopoly theory in *Principles*, and a lengthy review in *Industry and Trade* (published 1919) of British, German, and American monopolistic problems in transportation and the like, free competition or a reasonable facsimile thereof seems to have predominated in the world Marshall saw.

Marshall's handling of monopoly indicates what he evidently meant by competition. Primarily he meant, for any one firm, the discipline imposed by the presence or the potential appearance of other firms offering the same product or something very close to that product. He was aware that the product of Producer B might be slightly different from that of Producer A, but for the most part he brushed aside these differences. He treated A's product and B's as being effectively homogeneous. It was this uniformity which enabled him to regard A and B as members of the same "industry." And the industry concept was essential to Marshall's theory; analytically, he emphasized it much more than he did the individual firm within that industry.

Later on, Chamberlin reversed this emphasis—and the reversal is absolutely fundamental to the difference between Marshallian and Chamberlinian economics. Chamberlin stressed the importance of small differences between A's product and B's: they give A monopolistic power, and they give B monopolistic power, he said. Chamberlin did not initially intend to destroy the industry concept. But once you accept his emphasis on the significance of product differentiation, the industry concept (as we shall see) *is* destroyed.

Marshall's emphasis on industries fitted neatly into his initial supply-and-demand approach. His demand curve is an *industry* demand: it refers to total consumer demand for a given product, homogeneous or very nearly so from one supplier to the next. His supply curve refers similarly to *industry* supply. Marshall almost never used the demand curve concept with respect to the market facing the individual firm, although there is an interesting exception in a footnote on page 458 of *Principles*.

Marshall had a more fundamental reason for wanting to consider individual firms only within their industry setting: he thought the industry had an enduring quality which the firm lacked. He had a biological, life-cycle theory of the firm. He likened the individual firms comprising an industry to the

13

trees comprising a forest: at any particular point in time, some firms would be young and immature, others would be in their prime, still others close to decay and death. A newcomer firm, Marshall thought, would typically have costs above the industry average; it would become "efficient" only by gaining experience and maturity. Older firms tended to lose vitality, and here Marshall obviously was thinking of the firm in terms of the influence exerted by its human proprietor.

As a consequence of his life-cycle view, when Marshall needed to discuss the individual firm he often did so in terms of his "representative firm"—the firm that is typical or average for the industry at that point in the industry's history. The firms within a Marshallian industry were all effectively homogeneous in terms of the product they produced. But, being in different stages of their life cycles, they were *not* uniform in terms of production cost.

It is notable that Marshall's life-cycle and representative-firm ideas constitute *almost all* of his theory of the firm. Today "the theory of the firm" means, in essence, the proposition that each firm sums up its environment in demand-curve and cost-curve terms. Consequently, the firm is only "in equilibrium" when producing that output at which marginal cost has climbed to equality with marginal revenue, since that is the profit-maximizing output.

These ideas are almost entirely absent in Marshall. Their omission is striking, considering his emphasis on the analytic importance of the marginal concept and his handling of the industry situation in "equilibrium" terms. There is something approaching the now-conventional theory of the firm in Marshall's monopoly chapter; but Marshall, as earlier noted, did not attach special importance to monopoly situations. Certainly *Principles* contains little of pure competition theory. Marshall's freely competitive firms do not face perfectly price-elastic demand curves; and to judge by a passage on pages 374–75, they normally operate at a price above marginal cost.

Marshall's theory is undoubtedly deficient in its failure to include a more detailed account of the individual firm's situation. It left a gap which his successors had to fill. They filled it by developing the theory of pure competition.

Perhaps Marshall's work is incomplete because at this stage he simply was unable to sum up the elements of all he had observed within any "theory of the firm." In other words, it is at this point that he was defeated by the magnitude of the problems he had tackled.

One major stumbling block was the problem of "increasing returns"—meaning, of course, the situation in which the firm can reduce its per unit cost if it expands its output. This reduction in average cost is perhaps available only if the firm builds a larger and more efficient plant; such a "long-run" improvement in cost is usually what is meant by increasing returns in today's literature. But it may also be possible that the firm could reduce its unit cost even in the "short run" by an increase in output, typically because fixed overhead costs could then be spread over a larger number of units.

The analytic problem is this: If a firm faces an increasing-return opportunity, what barriers are there, if any, to stop or hinder the firm from seizing the opportunity? Pure competition theory says flatly that the only barrier is time. A purely competitive firm in these circumstances is "out of equilibrium," and it will expand its output with no more delay than the time needed to wear out an old plant and build a new one. When pure competition theory came under attack in the 1920s, it was precisely on this issue. It was argued that the increasing-return phenomenon was too commonplace to be accounted for in quite such cavalier fashion.

Both pure competition theory and the attack thereon

came, of course, long after Marshall had first puzzled over the increasing-returns matter. To judge by the space he devoted to it, Marshall also seems to have turned up many increasing-return cases in his inquiries, and he was not content with a casual explanation.

There are three parts to Marshall's interpretation. First, he said, some *apparent* opportunities may in fact be beyond the firm's grasp. If we look back at recent growth within some industry, and note how reductions in per-unit cost went hand-in-hand with increased size of plant for the various firms involved, we may be tempted to cite this as an instance of increasing returns to scale of plant. Actually, these cost economies may have opened up for each firm only because of improvements in the total *industry* environment, and only as a consequence of *industry* growth. Each firm had to keep more or less in step with other industry members in expansion. If so, this is an example of *external* economies resulting from greater *industry* output, and not a genuine example of internal-to-the-firm increasing returns to scale.

Second, Marshall said, genuine increasing-return opportunities might be slow of exploitation because of the firm's life span. Plant expansion must be undertaken gradually, and firms moving into the later and less vital stages of their life cycles will in due time lose the incentive for expansion.

Third, he added, a firm wanting to exploit such an opportunity would be slowed down by the difficulties of marketing all its extra output. And here, once again, is the puzzle of "what Marshall meant." If the marketing difficulty argument is framed in demand curve terms, it emerges as a downward-sloping, monopoly-like demand curve—which is exactly how Chamberlin interpreted it. Yet Marshall refused to concede that a firm's situation must be "monopolistic" because it has competitive difficulties in marketing extra output.

Whatever Marshall may have wanted to mean, our task here is to observe what he was interpreted by his successors as meaning—and here, the evidence is clear. His "free competition" was developed into pure competition, and his "monopolistic markets" became the theory of monopoly. Once these developments had occurred, the "cost controversy" broke out among economists—and when it did, the stage was set for Chamberlin's work. It is this cost controversy we must now consider as the final preliminary to Chamberlin himself.

2. PURE COMPETITION AND THE "COST CONTROVERSY"

When Marshall's "free competition" was interpreted as meaning pure competition, the result seemed to be much tighter integration of a rather loosely structured body of analysis. Marshall had not indicated clearly the exact relationship between his free competition and the supply-curve-and-demand-curve approach to price, perhaps because he was unable to decide how the two sets of ideas could be merged. (As already noted, he had to some degree inherited rather than developed the supply-and-demand approach.)

Pure competition theory *is* consistent with supply-and-demand treatment, simply because it provides a careful and detailed account of the supply curve's background. The short-run industry supply curve (as any of today's price theory texts will indicate) is the total of individual-firm supply curves. And the individual-firm supply curves come from their marginal cost curves, starting from a bottom point marked by the minimum level of average variable cost.

This account may or may not be an accurate description of events; it may or may not be what Marshall intended; but at least it is clear. In fact, it is so clear that it has become a standard for judging other would-be accounts. Nobody has yet managed to explain, with comparable precision, what the background of a supply curve is for any situation *other than* pure competition.

In short, the evolution of pure competition theory seemed to tie up a great many loose ends. It explained, in proper detail, what free competition could mean. It provided a theory of the firm which gave proper emphasis to the marginal elements whose importance Marshall had emphasized. And it fitted neatly into the industry supply-curve-and-demand-curve approach.

Moreover, pure competition theory is significant in that its basic characteristic is the exclusion of all monopoly elements. By an argument now conventionally accepted, any monopoly influence on price distorts the manner in which scarce resources are allocated. Hence the price and output quantity pattern that would result from pure competition in all industries is viewed (with some few qualifications that we need not consider here) as indicating a welfare "ideal." Yet simply because it *is* an ideal, pure competition theory's ability to describe *actual* competitive situations is, to say the least, in doubt.

Unfortunately, this is the crucial problem. In the course of tidying up analytic loose ends, and of spelling out a competitive ideal, the relevance of the theory to *actual* situations tended to be overlooked. Hence, once the equation between free competition and pure competition had been accomplished, the stage was set for an anti-Marshallian revolt. Marshall had been deeply anxious for theory to be disciplined by what he called "the actual facts"—yet his own theory, as later interpreted, was about to undergo attack for its failure to correspond with actual circumstances!

In retrospect, it is easy to see what happened. Despite his

contributions to economics, and his remarkable personal authority as teacher, Marshall's theory was in many respects quite insufficiently developed. His followers and successors were less cautious than Marshall; in their hands, a rather primitive analytic structure quickly hardened into dogma.

Objections to this dogma began with J. H. Clapham's article, "Of Empty Economic Boxes" (*Economic Journal*, 1922). Clapham's "boxes" were concepts in the economist's mind, in particular the concepts of increasing-return and decreasing-return industries which had been developed from Marshall's work. Are there real-life industries, Clapham asked, to which these designations apply? Open these conceptual "boxes," and do you find anything "real" inside them?

With this query, Clapham began the famous "cost controversy." There is space here to consider only what is, by common consent, the most forceful and influential contribution, Piero Sraffa's article in the 1926 *Economic Journal*, "The Laws of Return under Competitive Conditions."

We have already seen that supply-and-demand analysis, despite its status as the textbook introduction to *all* price situations, if taken literally, really applies only to the special case of pure competition (that being the only case in which the background of the supply curve can be explained). In brief, Sraffa's argument was this: 1) this supply-and-demand, pure-competition package relies excessively on the law of diminishing returns, while at the same time it is blind to the observed fact of *increasing* returns; 2) the resulting analysis is based on such restrictive assumptions as to have little application to real-life situations.

If we ask why a supply curve "rises" (runs from southwest to northeast), the answer is: diminishing returns. If output is increased, production must push harder against the fact of a limited resource stock, so per-unit cost rises. But, Sraffa noted, the diminishing-returns law had *not* been evolved with respect to such problems of cost and price. It had instead been introduced, especially by Ricardo, to show how the distribution of income between landowners and laborers would change as more and more labor was put to work on a fixed area of land. It was recognized that as the impact of diminishing returns was felt, the cost of the thing produced would be affected. But at least to a first approximation, all commodities (or all farm commodities) would be about *equally* affected, and so their relative prices would be unchanged.

Sraffa insisted that the diminishing-returns law had been carried into the quite different area of competitive price theory, for reasons of analytic convenience, without asking if the law would survive this transplanting. If a single competitive industry employed *all*, or even most, of the available supply of an input, then the diminishing-returns effect would be felt if industry output expanded. But when a single competitive industry needs more of an input, it can usually draw this supply from other industries, and the price of that input may not be significantly affected. We cannot argue that when *all* industries expand, the diminishing returns effect will appear, because that moves us out of the area chosen for competitive price analysis. It is Marshallian *ceteris paribus* analysis: the output of other industries is assumed constant.

At this stage, two points could be raised against Sraffa. First, at least in the short run, each firm's stock of plant and equipment is fixed, and this assures a diminishing returns effect (higher per-unit cost) if output is sufficiently increased. Second, concerning the long run, Sraffa's argument seems to say only that the long-run pure-competition supply curve is flat or approximately so.

But Sraffa then brought the second half of his argument

into play: pure competition's dismissal of the fact of *increasing* returns. According to this theory, no increasing-return opportunity can exist, save on a transitory basis. Its existence implies falling marginal cost, which in turn implies disequilibrium. A profit-maximizing firm in pure competition must push out along its perfectly flat demand curve, increasing its output and sales, until it reaches its equilibrium where marginal cost has *risen* to equality with market price.

Is this true of real life? "Everyday experience," Sraffa said, "shows that a very large number of undertakings—and the majority of those which produce manufactured consumer's goods—work under conditions of individual diminishing costs." Output is ordinarily restrained, not by rising per-unit cost, but by the difficulty of selling more goods. In sum, the assertions of pure competition theory clash with observed facts.

So we are back once again at Marshall's increasing-return problem. You will recall that Marshall cited the competitive difficulties of marketing extra output as one reason why an increasing-return opportunity would not be quickly exploited. But he would not describe such difficulties as "monopolistic" —in fact, he was sharply critical of Cournot's analysis of increasing returns because it suggested just such an association with monopoly.

In the post-Marshallian 1920s, it had become doctrine that in the truly "monopoly free" situation—pure competition— the firm has no marketing problems, for it can sell as much as it pleases at an established market price. So it is understandable that Sraffa felt impelled to tackle increasing returns in monopoly terms. In his oft-quoted words, "It is necessary, therefore, to abandon the path of free competition and turn in the opposite direction, namely, toward monopoly." (Sraffa's use of the term "free competition" is noteworthy. He was attacking *pure* competition; he accepted the convention that pure competition meant the same thing as Marshall's free competition.)

Sraffa not only attacked pure competition theory; he rejected the compromise idea that price theory should be made up of a *mixture* of competition and monopoly theories. This was an idea at which Marshall had hinted, especially in his final work, *Industry and Trade*. Sraffa wanted the whole structure of price theory built afresh in *monopoly* terms (and in general equilibrium terms, not *ceteris paribus* terms).

In economic theory, frontal attacks rarely succeed. Economists are not disposed to reject established theory, whatever its shortcomings, unless the attacker offers a reasonably detailed outline of the alternative theory he wants to be substituted. This Sraffa did not do, even though the closing pages of his article anticipate many of Chamberlin's ideas. In particular, Sraffa saw clearly that product differentiation could be interpreted as a monopolistic element.

In this sense, Sraffa's article fell short of its major objective. What Sraffa *did* accomplish was to intensify the growing dissatisfaction with orthodox price theory. The way was cleared for rapid and widespread acceptance of Chamberlin's work. For two reasons, Chamberlin's argument had far greater impact than Sraffa's. First, Chamberlin submitted a detailed, book-length outline of monopolistic competition theory. Second, he argued that his theory *was* a mixture of competitive and monopolistic elements. It was new; yet at the same time it did not seem to involve the violent break with established tradition which Sraffa's argument demanded.

It is worth recalling that Chamberlin's opposition to pure competition theory, considered as a description of real events, was just as vigorous as Sraffa's. The only difference was that Chamberlin saw *some* truth in pure competition theory. Moreover, as his views changed, Chamberlin's willingness to employ pure competition as an ingredient in his own theory diminished. At this later stage, Chamberlin's thinking came to bear a marked resemblance to that of Sraffa.

3. CHAMBERLIN: THE FOUNDATIONS

Our first task in evaluating Chamberlinian economics is to consider Chapters I through IV of *Monopolistic Competition*—particularly Chapter IV—for it is here that all of Chamberlin's basic ideas are set out.

Chapters I and II can be covered rapidly. Chapter I is important primarily as an introductory outline of the argument in Chapters III and IV. Chapter II deals with pure competition, the theory which Chamberlin wanted to unseat from its dominant position in price analysis. This was necessary material in 1933, but today it is familiar. Since it deals with ideas he wanted to revise rather than those he wished to advance, it is not of great significance with respect to Chamberlin's essential contribution.

Chapter III is the oligopoly chapter—much of it a review of the then-existing material on duopoly. Prior to 1933, the only approach toward oligopoly to have been examined at much length had been a special duopoly situation first devised by Cournot. There are two mineral springs. Their waters (presumably identical or almost so) are sold by the two owners. In given circumstances of demand and production cost, what will the resulting price be? Cournot had produced one solution, Bertrand a different one, Edgeworth still another—and so on. Chamberlin pointed out that the greater part of this work had overlooked one crucial fact: where there are only two sellers, or more generally where total numbers are small, then each seller will almost certainly discover that what *he* does affects

23

his competitors, and what *they* do affects him. The situation is one of mutual interdependence.

In these circumstances, if each seller recognizes the influence he has on price, direct and indirect, then even if there is no explicit or tacit agreement among the sellers, the resulting price will be "the monopoly price"—so Chamberlin said. In this he was relying, perhaps more than he first realized, on the special circumstances assumed in the Cournot case, for they are circumstances which make it fairly clear to suggest a "monopoly price" that exists independently of the presence of any monopoly firm. Unfortunately, it *is* a very special case, and oligopoly analysis becomes much more difficult once it is left behind.

We have to keep Chamberlin's contribution in proper perspective. Today, when the ideas of oligopoly and mutual interdependence are familiar, it is difficult to appreciate what an advance it was merely to have brought these ideas successfully to the attention of economists, and to have done so almost single-handed. Morever, he had put his finger on the essential property of oligopoly situations: mutual interdependence. What Chamberlin did not do, as has already been noted, was to produce a *theory* of oligopoly. For such a theory, developing his basic idea, he would have had to demonstrate that something which may be called "the monopoly price" exists even when no monopoly control over supply exists, in circumstances more general than those of the Cournot case. Having isolated this price, he would have had to show, with respect to supply offered by a small (oligopoly) group, that each group member could fairly readily identify this price, without too much likelihood of disagreement. Morever, he would further have had to show that it would be in the separate profit-maximizing interest of each group member to maintain that price—that each would get a sufficient share of the business available, and so would not want to use a different price.

We may speculate that even in 1933 Chamberlin was quite aware that he had left a great deal unsaid in the matter of oligopoly, and yet was not overly concerned, considering it a task for later attention. It is reasonably clear that he felt he had much more to say, initially at any rate, about the significance and implications of product differentiation than he had about oligopoly.

Product differentiation is the central idea in Chapter IV. When he reached the fifth edition of *Monopolistic Competition* in 1946, and was adding an extra chapter, Chamberlin wryly quoted a comment made to him by a student: "Chapter IV is easy—you don't say anything in it" (p. 204). The student was wrong, for the core of Chamberlin's thinking is in that chapter.

Had the comment been that there is very little *theory* in Chapter IV, it would have been correct. The basic raw material of theory is there. But theory means the refinement of basic ideas, and the resolution of mutually inconsistent ideas, to the point that one knows what one must accept and what one must reject if one is to commit oneself to those ideas. It means the development of basic material to the stage where a series of propositions emerges that can be tested against experience— and, in the process of such testing, contradicted should that prove necessary. If there is no opportunity of contradiction, then there is no theory. Chamberlin's theory is in Chapters V and VII (which we shall discuss in the next section), not in Chapter IV.

Chamberlin stuck to most of the basic ideas of chapter IV —the ideas, not yet theory—throughout his work. The ideas are these: that virtually all real competitive situations involve a mixture of competitive and monopoly elements; that pure competition theory taken alone is consequently a bad description of actual events; that differentiation of products is the key to a theory combining monopoly and competitive elements; that virtually all products are differentiated; and that the analytic consequence of any differentiated product is a tilted demand curve facing its seller.

It is essential to an understanding of Chamberlin's work to grasp that when he spoke of "monopolistic competition" he was as likely as not to be speaking of these basic ideas rather than the theory into which they were to be worked. It is equally essential to note that of the many provocative ideas in *Monopolistic Competition*, some undergo lengthy translation into theory, while others are only partly worked, and still others are left almost untouched.

It is this matter of uneven development of ideas that explains why the textbook version of "monopolistic competition" is so much narrower than Chamberlin's own. The large-group case is unquestionably the case most thoroughly worked out in *Monopolistic Competition*; it is carried to the point of diagrammatic illustration. Consequently the profession tagged it "monopolistic competition," somewhat to Chamberlin's annoyance. Of course, he to some extent defeated his own intention that the term should have the broadest possible application when he introduced the word "oligopoly" with respect to small-group cases.

The awkward thing is that "monopolistic competition" can thus be interpreted in any of three ways. It can mean 1) the broadly ranging set of *ideas* presented in chapters I and IV (which is what Chamberlin often means); 2) the specific large-group and small-group *theories* worked out, to at least some degree, in *Monopolistic Competition* (which is what he sometimes may mean); or 3) the large-group theory (which is what the textbooks mean).

One example may illustrate how troublesome this can become. In his opening attack on homogeneous-product or pure competition in chapter I, Chamberlin points out that there is competition to which this theory is blind, the competition between physically diverse products—housing space and automobiles, for example. And there is such competition in the minds of consumers who must choose between a larger apartment and a larger car. But Chamberlin's remarks infer that monopolistic competition extends, via the concept of product differences, even to diverse-product competition such as this —and it does, by interpretation 1 above. However, there is no real diverse-product competition in the *theory* of monopolistic competition as outlined in chapters v through vii—i.e., by interpretation 3. Almost certainly, the "close substitutes" discussed in those chapters must be physically similar. How else can you speak (as Chamberlin did) of "uniform" demand curves and cost curves, as among the competing producers? Stigler seized on this fact in his *Five Lectures on Economic Problems*, one of the best-known criticisms of monopolistic competition. He pointed out that the competition described in chapters v through vii *cannot* involve really diverse products, or else much of Chamberlin's discussion becomes meaningless. In sum, interpretation 3 (theory) did not live up to all the promises of interpretation 1 (ideas).

We cannot say that Chamberlin thereupon discarded the idea of diverse-product competition. In *General Theory of Value*, published after Stigler's criticism, he says that monopolistic competition "includes *all* competition" (p. 44, italics added). It would be more correct to say—and this of course is the interesting thing—that he discarded much of the theory of chapters v through vii. By "monopolistic competition" he meant that general set of ideas which he was confident would one day receive adequate expression in the form of theory.

27

The idea that actual competition is typically a mixture of monopoly and competition was not original with Chamberlin. Marshall had said as much in *Industry and Trade*. But *how* do the ingredients blend? Where is the theory in which they are suitably mixed? This is the problem of conversion of ideas into theory which Chamberlin faced; and there is only a little exaggeration in saying that all of his work is principally a struggle to furnish an adequate and internally consistent answer to such questions.

Chamberlin began by isolating the "pure" extremes of monopoly and competition. Chapter iv makes the point that although pure competition can reasonably be designated as monopoly-free, it cannot be said that monopoly is competition-free—not as the word "monopoly" is customarily used. The ordinary monopolist sells one single product only, and by definition, there is no other seller offering a product that is identical or even a close substitute. The monopoly firm is accordingly free of competition in this particular form. But this does not necessarily mean at all that it is completely free of competition, that it must have some protected or walled-off market to be exploited at will. The monopoly firm still must face competition from the sellers of different products also in search of the consumer's dollar. Housing and automobiles are quite different products; yet housing may still compete with automobiles in the consumer's budget decision, just as butter may compete with oleomargarine. So long as consumer incomes are limited, some products must be rejected. It is much too easy, in evaluating the monopoly situation, to make the mistake of describing it solely in terms of *particularly successful monopolies*. The fact that a firm is offering a product for which there are no close substitutes at all is no guarantee whatsover that this firm will earn above-normal profits. In particular cases, in fact, that firm may be unable even to survive against the competition of different but more attractive products. In Marshallian terminology, there is inter-industry competition as well as intra-industry competition. If we want to conceive of a monopoly situation, Chamberlin said, in which there is literally no competition at all, then we must visualize not "ordinary monopoly" but a monopoly firm controlling the supply of *all* the available products. This competition-free situation Chamberlin defined as *pure* monopoly—the counterpart of pure competition, which is totally free of monopoly elements.

Define the extremes in this way, and at least three alternative paths thereupon open up for the development of monopolistic competition. First, considering the essential feature of pure monopoly, we might think that the typical intermediate and real-life situation that results when we mix it with pure competition would be a case in which each firm controls the supply of *several* products. But that is not Chamberlin's path, of course; in fact, the idea has never seemed sufficiently promising to be used as the basis of a general theory.

Second, if we add rather more of the purely competitive ingredient, the intermediate result might be the ordinary monopolist—monopolist in his control of *one* product, competitive in facing other products. Had Chamberlin chosen to develop monopolistic competition in this way, he would of course have followed the Sraffa monopoly path; and his development of diverse-product competition might have protected him against the Stigler criticism.

As we shall see, Chamberlin later turned in this direction. But in the beginning of his work (specifically, on p. 68), this path is rejected. It is rejected because of the inability of ordinary monopoly theory to take proper account of *close* competitive relationships.

In other words, Chamberlin chose a third path—not several-product monopoly, not single-product monopoly, but a mixture containing even more of the purely competitive ingredient than the ordinary single-product monopoly situation implies.

Before we look more closely at this third path, it is interesting to observe why Chamberlin picked it. Sraffa, recall, was significantly anti-Marshallian. And Sraffa's ordinary monopoly path would have been considerably more anti-Marshallian than Chamberlin—initially, at any rate—wanted to be. In one critical respect, Chamberlin *had* to break away from Marshallian ideas. Once this break had been accomplished, he then wanted to make his analysis as conventional as it could possibly be made.

The break with Marshall involved the idea of "product." Despite his occasional references to special products and special markets, Marshall almost always thought of the product in *industry* terms. Were he to have spoken of soap, he would have meant *soap*, not Ivory soap nor Palmolive soap. *Chamberlin applied the product concept explicitly to the individual firm.* That was his basic innovation: each firm's product was different.

By this concept of differentiation, Chamberlin (along with Sraffa) swung attention away from the industry and towards the firm. But every innovation has its cost. Chamberlin had gained new freedom to tackle his problems, but he had to answer the question: what happens to the concept of "industry"? Is there still such a thing, when each firm now has its own specific market, and is cut loose from the bonds of product homogeneity by means of which the industry had hitherto been defined?

Had Chamberlin brushed the industry concept aside, he would have rejected the greater part of Marshallian analysis—and he had no plans to be that much of a revolutionary. He had locked the door on the idea of Marshall's homogeneous products, but he chose instead something as close to it as he could reasonably get, namely the idea of "close substitutes," in close competition with one another. In place of the industry, he introduced "the group."

Chamberlin nowhere defines his "group" (beyond saying at a later date, in *General Theory of Value*, that it was "always meant to be a completely flexible concept"). But we have already noted that Chamberlin's "close substitutes" must be physically similar products—in fact he says so on page 81. So we can conclude that his "group" is a close substitute for the Marshallian industry (the use of a different term perhaps being appropriate in a work dedicated to the importance of product differentiation). Evidently Chamberlin took for granted, as Marshall before him had done on many occasions, that his readers would know what he meant.

So the theory of monopolistic competition is, or at any rate begins as, a theory of competition within a group of producers, each of them offering a close substitute for the products of the others. These products are differentiated, and the result is a monopoly-like demand curve facing each seller. This "third path" which Chamberlin chose is really a mixture of *ordinary* monopoly and pure competition, for the element of pure monopoly is hardly recognizable therein.

By sticking as closely to Marshallian ideas as he could, Chamberlin became exposed to the criticism that his theory did not take account of the automobiles-versus-housing kind of competition as he had initially suggested it would. Yet he was adhering to Marshall in a different sense. Marshall's *Principles* carries the motto *Natura non facit saltum* on its title page, and it is true that no major work in economics, not even Keynes's *General Theory*, has ever managed to jump completely away from its predecessors to make a fresh start. Chamberlin's work was acclaimed because of its provocative new ideas; but it was acclaimed also because the development of these ideas drew heavily on established doctrine. Moreover, there was always the hope that the theory could encompass diverse-product competition at a later stage in its development.

Had Chamberlin tackled a theory of oligopoly, then he would have had to break into fresher and more controversial ground; but this he did not do. Of course, in Chapters v through vii—which we are about to consider—there is some discussion of the oligopoly case (particularly in Sections 4 and 5 of Chapter v). But in matters of theory, this material is not so much an enlargement of the ideas expressed in Chapter iii as a reiteration of them. The real development of earlier material in the later chapters takes place with respect to the large-group case. It is here that Chamberlin evidently felt (initially, at least) that he could most successfully blend pure competition and monopoly theories.

4. THE TEXTBOOK THEORY

Chapters v through vii of *Monopolistic Competition* outline Chamberlin's actual *theory*. They are detail-filled chapters, so it is well to note that the basic skeleton is a simple one. It is a theory of *equilibrium positions*. Chamberlin tackles first the *firm*. The firm has three variables under its control (changes in price, in product variety, and in selling expenditure), and it manipulates these variables in search of a maximum-profit equilibrium position. Then Chamberlin tackles *group equilibrium:* first the large group, then (briefly) the small (oligopoly) group.

All this analysis is conducted in Marshallian, *ceteris paribus* terms. The *ceteris paribus* method is awkward when the firm has as many as three variables to handle, and so the sales expenditure topic is deferred. In chapter v, really the key chapter in this section, the firm deals with the other two variables only. Chapter VI is an introductory discussion of sales expenditure. Then chapter VII repeats chapter V, with the third variable added. (The seven section titles within chapter VII are almost identical with those of chapter V.)

Before we consider these matters in more detail, there is one essential fact which is often ignored yet is basic to a proper evaluation of the theory—and is indeed basic if one is to grasp the nature of the clash between pure and monopolistic competition theories. The fact is this: each theory implicitly assumes a different type of sales market.

Many of the conditions of pure competition are satisfied if the market type corresponds to any of the farm-product exchanges such as those of the Chicago Board of Trade, or to any of the major stock exchanges. If you sell on such a market, you face something very close to the perfectly price-elastic demand curve of pure competition. Each such market has an elaborate set of institutions designed to absorb changes in supply (or demand) with minimal change in price. Your supply must be very large indeed before it affects price perceptibly. You cannot bargain on such markets, and there are no problems of "competition" in the ordinary sense. It is pointless to engage in sales effort, for you can sell as much as you please at an established price, or something very close to the price for that day. The only decision you can make concerns the quantity you wish to sell (or buy).

Marshall called these markets "highly organized." For our purposes, the term "organized" seems more appropriate, to contrast them with the *unorganized* markets of everyday experience.

In the *unorganized* market, each supplying firm, whether manufacturer, wholesaler, or retailer, must hunt up its own customers—or the buyer must hunt up his own seller. These are the markets in which almost all supplying firms find themselves engaged; and common experience tells us that they do not face anything resembling a perfectly elastic demand curve. These are the markets in which increasing-return opportunities may be slow of exploitation because the output-expanding firm must reckon with the competition of rival firms. They are the markets in which products are differentiated from one seller to the next (whereas in organized markets, products *must* be homogeneous as between any two sellers). In sum, unorganized markets are the markets in which pure competition theory seems a very awkward fit indeed.

In any such unorganized market, no supplying firm can make a decision directly as to the output quantity it proposes to sell. This decision can be made only indirectly, and to this end, the firm has three variables open to it: 1) alter price; 2) make its product "different" from those of competing firms; and 3) engage in selling expenditure.

These are of course precisely the variables with which Chamberlin endows his firms. They would be meaningless if the firm sold on an organized exchange. Hence—although Chamberlin never said this—we can conclude that monopolistic competition theory was theory constructed to fit the conditions of unorganized markets. And with this established, we must at once ask: does it fit in *all* critical respects?

The almost-perfectly elastic demand curve facing any organized-market seller illustrates *one* critical difference between the two market types—the one on which Chamberlin anchored his theory. But *another* difference, which Chamberlin initially ignored, was the much greater tendency of unorganized markets to produce oligopolistic behavior (for reasons we shall shortly consider). When in due course he became aware of this, Chamberlin had to try to recast his theory.

What Chamberlin did initially was to seize on the unorganized-market phenomenon of product differentiation. This, he said, is a monopoly element: it results in a monopoly-like demand curve facing each individual seller. And Chamberlin had sufficient confidence in the vital significance of this *one* element that he then began his outline of monopolistic competition theory with a model *which was as close to pure competition as it could possibly be made.*

With the benefit of hindsight, we can say that this choice of a starting point provoked much of the misunderstanding over monopolistic competition theory about which Chamberlin was subsequently to complain. Chapter v includes a warning that this model is only a starting point, and is not representative of the full-fledged theory of monopolistic competition. Yet the material which follows in the chapter is developed in such a way that the warning becomes completely obscured.

The starting point in question is "the uniformity case": each member firm within the group has precisely the same demand curve and cost curves as every other producer. Now monopolistic competition stresses the individuality and uniqueness of each separate producer. A case in which they are exactly *alike* in the critical consideration of demand and cost curves hardly seems representative. Chamberlin recognizes this: he says the uniformity assumption is "heroic," and only temporary.

Why should he begin in this curious way? To answer, we must first note Chamberlin's outline of equilibrium for the individual firm, in section 2 of chapter v. With selling expenditure postponed (for chapter vii), and for any given product variety, *price* is the variable the firm can manipulate. Since the demand curve is monopoly-like, all that is needed to describe the firm's equilibrium position is the elementary theory of profit-maximizing monopoly.

In section 3, Chamberlin turns to *group* equilibrium (more specifically, large-group equilibrium). Here, the uniformity assumption first appears: all firms in the group are exactly alike. The result is a sudden jump from monopoly theory for the individual firm to something which might very well be pure competition theory for the group. Since all firms have the same demand and cost curves, all charge the same price—the "market price." If one firm just breaks even, all do; if one firm is earning profits or incurring a loss, all are. If the overall experience is one of profit, new firms will be attracted and will enter the group; if of loss, some existing firms must be driven out. The discussion goes on to consider possible external economies or diseconomies, should the size and output of the group expand. All this runs exactly as it would in pure competition, and it might well come from a textbook outline of that situation.

Chamberlin even borrows a "diffusion effect" from pure competition. The diffusion effect is the large-group effect: if one supplier within the group changes his price and sales quantity, the effect is so diffused among the other suppliers that nobody feels the change perceptibly; there is no oligopolistic interaction. Now this is a legitimate assumption if one is discussing pure competition as it would operate in the conditions of an organized market. In any such market, it is almost impossible for any change in *my* supply quantity to affect significantly any other single supplier. But in an unorganized market, there is absolutely no mechanism to promise any diffusion effect. If I change my price or my sales expenditure, my *closest* competitors may be perceptibly affected, and they may retaliate with a counter-competitive move which affects *my* market. In sum, the diffusion assumption is *not* legitimate with respect to the type of market Chamberlin was discussing, and we shall see in due course how much trouble this was to cause him.

Why did Chamberlin use the uniformity case? Almost

certainly, because he wanted to begin in the closest possible proximity to familiar and well-established territory. To be sure, he intended to *attack* pure competition theory. But he had established the *monopoly* characteristic of his individual group member—the monopoly-like demand curve. With this difference established, he felt he could then borrow some enemy territory, at least temporarily, as a kind of launching platform for his own theory. He was simply introducing the "competitive element" which he had said at the outset his theory would contain.

Chamberlin was sufficiently aware of the potential danger in the uniformity case to include various warnings as to its non-representative quality. His Figure 14 (p. 91) shows the demand curve for "the general class of product" (what in Marshallian or pure competition terms would be industry demand). On the same page is a footnote warning that the idea of such a demand curve is not very reliable in the circumstances of monopolistic competition. On pages 81–82, just as he is about to develop his analysis of group equilibrium, he warns that monopolistic competition "to a very considerable extent . . . defies comprehensive description as a 'group' problem." But despite these cautions, he *did* use the group concept and he *did* use the uniformity model.

The "uniformity case" might have caused no trouble had Chamberlin gone on to develop adequately "the diversity case," which drops the assumption of all-alike demand and cost curves and so can be considered a true outline of monopolistic competition. This Chamberlin did not do. Almost all his discussion of group equilibrium runs in uniformity terms. The diversity situation gets four pages in chapter v and just over one page in chapter vii. Within those pages, most of the discussion is concerned with the single fact that, in diversity, profits will not be uniformly eliminated by entry of new competitors, as in the uniformity case. Some strategically placed firms may then be able to retain part of their "above-normal" profit.

Now profit retention deserves recognition as an important aspect of diversity, and the textbooks are usually faithful to Chamberlin in reporting it. But if it is the *only* significant difference, then it appears that monopolistic competition, *even in its fully developed form*, strongly resembles pure competition. If we add to this the fact that Chamberlin begins chapters v through vii by talking about "close substitutes," the full threat to his theory suddenly emerges. With "close substitutes" involved, is the departure from perfectly elastic demand of much consequence? If the demand curve facing the firm is *almost* flat, monopolistic competition is not really worth much attention as a separate theory. We reach the verdict on monopolistic competition pronounced in the textbook quotations cited on page 1 of this study.

These considerations do not constitute any victory for pure competition theory. They tell us only that Chamberlin underestimated the task of producing significantly *different* theory; in section 5, we must consider his second attempt. It is interesting to note that at this earlier stage he took so much for granted a *marked* departure from perfect price elasticity of demand, that he did not even raise the question. It is not mentioned until late in chapter vii, and then only incidentally to a quite different topic. Chamberlin there says (p. 166) that cases of near-perfect elasticity for the firm "must be very unusual."

Chamberlin's emphasis on the uniformity case produced other misinterpretations. In particular, he later expressed his distress concerning overemphasis on "the tangency equilibrium." This is the familiar textbook case in which the firm winds up in final equilibrium with its monopoly-like demand curve just *touching* the U-shaped average cost curve. Competition (provided if necessary by entry of new firms) has squeezed profit down to that "normal profit" level needed to persuade the firm to stay in business. Since the demand curve is tilted, the tangency equilibrium point cannot possibly be at the *bottom* of the U-shaped average cost curve. The more the "tilt" of the demand curve, the farther from the bottom point this tangency point must be.

This "tangency equilibrium" case offers (or rather, seems to offer) an explanation of the Marshall–Sraffa phenomenon of increasing returns (decreasing cost). Unquestionably, this explains much of the attention which has been paid to Chamberlin's tangency equilibrium. It is now part of the standard textbook outline of monopolistic competition. Moreover, a comparison is often made in such texts with the equilibrium of *pure* competition, where the firm winds up with its perfectly flat demand curve just tangent to the average cost curve at the bottom (lowest-cost level) of that cost curve. It is then concluded that monopolistic competition is "inefficient," since price and per-unit cost are higher than they would be in pure competition.

It has been argued, notably by Donald Dewey and Harold Demsetz, that (whatever the true explanation of Sraffa's phenomenon may be) imperfect or monopolistic competition does not necessarily result in such inefficiency. And what must be stressed here is that Chamberlin might well agree with the Dewey–Demsetz view. The tangency solution emerges *only* in the special and nonrepresentative "uniformity case."

Moreover, Chamberlin did not have in mind the welfare conclusion that pure competition is "better," by the standard of the resulting price and per-unit cost. He made the comparison between pure and monopolistic competition tangency equilibria himself, but only to make the point that monopolistic competition is *different*. By his standard—the standard of descriptive accuracy—it is monopolistic competition that comes off as "better." It gives a more accurate description of "the way things are," and unavoidably must be, in his view.

No attempt is made here to outline everything Chamberlin said in chapters v through vii, since that would largely repeat what is to be found in any textbook. It must suffice to summarize briefly what Chamberlin had to say about the large-group uniformity case, the large-group diversity case, and the small-group case.

In the large-group uniformity case, as already indicated, all firms wind up charging the same price, in "tangency" positions, earning only normal competitive profit. Price is higher than it would be under pure competition, because of the location of the tangency point on the cost curve (not at its bottom point). When he reaches chapter vii, Chamberlin notes that pure competition theory *doubly* understates the actual tendency of prices, first because it understates actual production cost, second because it assumes zero selling cost. Perhaps it does not do too much injustice to chapter vii, which is a long chapter, to say that its principal conclusions are these: firms *do* engage in selling expenditure, and these sales outlays have to find their way into market price charged.

In the large-group diversity case, equilibrium conditions are not quite so clear. Some firms may wind up as in uniformity, earning only normal competitive profit; more successful firms earn higher profit and charge somewhat higher prices. It is interesting to note that while Chamberlin *attacks* pure competition theory, he also *needs* that theory, as a standard of comparison. His conclusions are clearest when his theory is closest to pure competition theory.

Conclusions are even more uncertain in the small-group, oligopoly case. Chamberlin does not carry his analysis much beyond the ideas already suggested in chapter iii. Price will land somewhere between an upper limit of "the monopoly price" (if sellers take full account of their influence on price) and a lower limit corresponding to price in the large-group uniformity case (if sellers fail to realize their mutual interdependence and their common power to influence price, and behave as though they were members of a large group).

There is a noteworthy property about Chamberlin's oligopoly discussion: it reads almost exactly as though pure (homogeneous-product) oligopoly were involved. Naturally, Chamberlin (believing that differentiation is all-pervasive) insists that his topic is differentiated-product oligopoly. Yet for practical purposes it is still pure oligopoly—and this for two reasons. First, all of Chamberlin's oligopoly discussion runs in terms of the uniformity case, which, as earlier indicated, runs as close as possible to homogeneity. Second, once the small-group case is reached, differentiation becomes less necessary as a monopoly element. Each small-group supplier can influence market price even if his product is undifferentiated.

Chamberlin is able to evolve his upper-limit monopoly price only by sticking rigidly to the uniformity assumption and by interpreting it in terms very close to product homogeneity. Assume there are five sellers, each of whom has exactly one-fifth of the total market demand at each and any price. Assume also that each firm has exactly the same marginal and average cost curves as the other four. Then each can compute its maximum-profit equilibrium position in simple monopoly terms. Each will wish to charge the same price—the monopoly price. But these are very demanding assumptions; and the moment they are relaxed in the slightest, the idea of a unique "monopoly price" begins to disintegrate.

In the course of Chamberlin's rather brief discussion of oligopoly, he includes two characteristically Chamberlinian ideas—each perceptive and thought-provoking, but each seeming to endanger the analysis which surrounds it. First, he suggests that what may *appear* to be a large group may in fact be an aggregation of small subgroups. Does this mean that the conclusions of large-group analysis do not necessarily apply in what seem to be large-group cases?

Second, Chamberlin observes that a group of firms may tacitly decide to accept a certain price and to compete in other ways. This idea is, of course, in general harmony with his discussion of competition via selling expenditure, yet there is no *theory* of price agreement in chapters v to vii, no account of the terms of possible agreement. In fact, the idea of such agreement calls into question the theory earlier spelled out. The one vital ingredient in Chamberlin's theory is the firm's monopoly-like demand curve; and a firm which abides by some price agreement is *not* taking advantage of that demand curve, but instead is behaving differently. Once again, the *idea* is there, but it is not developed into theory—at least not at this point. But there is more of Chamberlin's work to consider; and both of these comments, as we shall see, prove to have more significance than their almost casual mention in chapter v would suggest.

Chapter vii ended the first two editions of *Monopolistic Competition*. How are we to sum up Chamberlin's contribution at this stage in the development of his work?

He had pushed the whole of price analysis a major step toward that descriptive realism which had been so sorely lacking in post-Marshallian theory—if only because he reviewed situations in which firms must compete on price, or through selling expenditures. Competition, he had made it apparent, can mean something much broader than "pure competition." Even the monopoly firm (he had made clear) may face such intense competition from other, different products that it may earn no profit, or may even be pushed into losses.

But the *theory* of monopolistic competition is at this stage unsatisfactory. Most obviously, Chamberlin faced the task of rewriting it to avoid the charge that it was only a minor variant of pure competition. This, it seemed, called for de-emphasis of "the uniformity case," and proper expansion of "the diversity situation."

Unfortunately, any such expansion would only uncover a basic flaw in Chamberlin's theory. His vision of monopolistic competition, in chapters v to vii, we know, had been this: firms within a *group* are in close competition with one another, yet each firm makes its own autonomous decisions on price, sales expenditure, and product variety in terms of its own *ceteris paribus* demand curve. A good case can be made that in all this Chamberlin was trying to merge two incompatible ideas—and the history of Chamberlin's subsequent work strengthens this case. A firm capable of making its decisions in terms of any such demand curve is *not* truly a member of any close-substitutes competitive group in the sense that membership significantly constrains its behavior. A firm truly a member of such a group *cannot* isolate its own market—the business it would lose with a price rise, the business it would gain with a reduction—in this *ceteris paribus* demand curve fashion.

The example of pure competition seems to say that marriage between individual-firm demand curve idea and group idea *is* possible; that is why Chamberlin borrowed from it. But pure competition is a very special case. Outside of the organized markets where its reasoning is valid, pure competition theory comes under attack precisely because of its assertion about the individual firm's demand curve.

So long as monopolistic competition theory sticks to the uniformity case, this underlying clash is concealed. If all firms have identical demand and cost curves, and consequently all ask the same price and sell the same output, the simple fact of their identity makes them a group by definition. But in what sense are they a group when we move on to the diversity case? Any equality of price or output is then a coincidence. It will not do to argue that they are still a group "because their products are close substitutes." What does the idea of "close substitutes" *mean*? What *constraint* does the close-substitute fact impose on each separate firm? We cannot just say that the effect of such competition is to push each group member's demand curve leftward, for that also happens to monopoly firms (who presumably are not group members) by reason of the competition they encounter.

In pure competition, each firm *knows* what group membership means: it means the constraint imposed by a common market price which it cannot alter. Is there any equivalent constraint in monopolistic competition?

Alternatively, suppose a firm *is* a group member, even though its product is sufficiently different to give it some degree of "monopoly" independence of price policy. Does this endow the firm with a *ceteris paribus* demand curve? The idea of such a curve is operationally meaningful only if, as the firm seeks its equilibrium position thereon, its own moves do not precipitate a shift in the demand curve's position. If the firm is protected by the diffusion effect which operates automatically in an organized market, there will be no shift; that is why Chamberlin assumed a diffusion effect. But he was writing theory for unorganized markets, in which there is no justification for assuming a diffusion effect, other than analytic convenience. Typically, in the unorganized market, as the firm gropes toward its equilibrium, its moves will affect some "close" competitors, who respond with countermoves—which shift the first firm's demand curve. The firm's situation is one of oligopolistic interdependence. All monopolistic competition situations are potentially or actually oligopolistic, and the problem is: what kind of behavior must we then look for in the firm?

The history of Chamberlin's subsequent work is the record of his discovery of these facts and his attempt to cope with them.

5. THE RECONSIDERATION

Chapter IX, "The Difference Between Monopolistic and Imperfect Competition," was added to *Monopolistic Competition* in 1946. As the title suggests, a part of it—but only a part—deals with Mrs. Robinson's work. Chamberlin devoted considerable time to a demonstration that his own analysis differed from Mrs. Robinson's, and we may lament that he did not turn at least part of these energies to more positive use.

Much of *Monopolistic Competition* does correspond with Mrs. Robinson's *The Economics of Imperfect Competition*, for their topics at least overlap. Triffin, in *Monopolistic Competition and General Equilibrium Theory*, devotes four pages to parallel quotations from the two books. Nevertheless, Mrs. Robinson's book is a book on monopoly, largely prompted by Sraffa's call for a turn towards monopoly. In contrast to Chamberlin, Mrs. Robinson spends almost no time on oligopoly; she recognizes the problem, then brushes it aside. As her book proceeds, it becomes more and more (to quote her own opening words) "a box of tools." The tools are those of monopoly analysis. With them she is able to show, for example, how price differentiation can be analyzed in monopoly terms. This is a particular instance of a monopoly firm *exploiting* its position, and exploitation, particularly the exploitation of labor, was Mrs. Robinson's special interest. She repeatedly trends off into such special topics, rather than sticking to the main task of theory applicable to the whole range of competitive situations, as Chamberlin tried to do.

Perhaps this dismisses Mrs. Robinson's work too summarily. But our present concern is with Chamberlin's chapter ix, and one thing is clear: the parts thereof dealing with Mrs. Robinson are of limited interest—whereas other parts, responding to critical comment, are deeply important.

Chapter ix begins with an attempt to dispel some "misconceptions" about monopolistic competition. First, Chamberlin insists that the technical devices of marginal revenue and marginal cost curves (emphasized by Mrs. Robinson) have no special place in his theory. Although *Monopolistic Competition* makes little use of the marginal concepts, Chamberlin's firms are exactly the same profit-maximizers as Mrs. Robinson's, and whether or not one uses the marginal curves to explain the nature of the profit-maximizing equilibrium is largely a matter of choice.

Chamberlin continues by deploring the overemphasis given "the tangency equilibrium." This tangency outcome *had* been overstressed by Chamberlin's readers, but he is not blameless, for the tangency outcome derives from "the uniformity case" which occupies almost all of chapters v to vii.

In sum, misconceptions such as these are not matters of vital concern. But Chamberlin then turns to the "misconceptions" arising out of the critical work of Nicholas Kaldor, and here we reach matters of real consequence.

Kaldor's articles are in the 1934 and 1935 volumes of *Economica.* The first reviewed Mrs. Robinson's book; the second developed the ideas of the first and turned them toward Chamberlin's work. Kaldor did not oppose the idea of a theory of imperfect or monopolistic competition; he was instead fully persuaded of the need for such theory. But he spared neither Mrs. Robinson nor Chamberlin when he felt they had been derelict in its construction. He was probing for the *sources* of competitive imperfection, and thought they lay mainly in two factors: "institutional monopoly," and economies of scale.

One example will illustrate the impact of Kaldor's argument. When Chamberlin was outlining his uniformity case, and had turned to group entry, he had specified that "the entry of new producers into the field in general and every portion of it in particular is free and unimpeded." One would not suspect the presence of any time-bomb buried in this innocent sentence. But Kaldor pointed out that such unimpeded entry must imply freedom on the part of an entering firm to *duplicate* the product of an existing producer. This is a vital thrust against the idea of the *uniqueness* of each separate producer. (Chamberlin took *that* sentence out of *Monopolistic Competition* at the same time as he added chapter IX.)

Kaldor went on to say that in fact duplication may be prevented by "institutional monopoly"—trademarks, copyright laws, and the like; these, he noted, Chamberlin had recognized. But Chamberlin had cited trademarks and copyrights as particular *instances* of product differentiation, and certainly had not intended the entire differentiation phenomenon to rest on the narrow foundation of institutional monopoly.

Matters were not much improved by Kaldor's proposal of a second base: economies of scale. He said that (with institutional monopoly absent) if "constant returns to scale" prevailed (if small firms could operate with equal cost efficiency, no matter how small they might be), there would be perfect (pure) competition. Whether or not this is so is a question we need not explore here. What matters is that even if we add "increasing returns to scale" to institutional monopoly, the resulting base for monopolistic competition is still a limited one. Unquestionably, Chamberlin had in mind a far broader base. (He did not use the idea of unorganized markets, but he was almost certainly thinking of the fact that there is product differentiation in every such market.)

Consider the threat to monopolistic competition implicit in Kaldor's argument. Suppose there is a situation in which economies of scale are minor, and the number of firms is large. Then (if institutional monopoly elements are absent), conditions will be *close* to perfect competition. We are back at an earlier point: if monopolistic competition differs only slightly from pure competition, is the difference so very important?

As Kaldor proceeded, the threat to monopolistic competition theory became increasingly dangerous. For Kaldor went on to attack the diffusion assumption which, as has already been pointed out, was a major defect in Chamberlin's theory. It simply is not appropriate in markets where firms compete via price, selling effort, and product variation. Yet the *ceteris paribus* demand curve relies on the diffusion assumption; and this demand curve is basic in the theory of chapters v through VII.

Now the problems which Kaldor had raised are in large part the same problems detailed at the close of section 4 in this essay, and the position into which they forced Chamberlin has already been indicated therein. To put matters bluntly, he had underestimated the difficulties in constructing a theory of monopolistic competition. It was imperative that he should move his analysis farther away from pure competition theory; having initially drawn too heavily on that theory, he now had to avoid the charge that his material was not significantly different therefrom. But this removal called for a much more comprehensive account of the nature of monopolistic competition theory—the theory, not the ideas—indicating what it did involve, and what it did not.

We can appreciate most easily how Chamberlin met this crisis by referring back to the point made earlier, that as soon as he had said monopolistic competition involved a "mix" of monopoly and competition elements, he then had a choice of three paths: several-product monopoly for each firm, single-product monopoly, or single-product monopoly with firms involved in *group* competition because their products are close substitutes for one another. Chamberlin picked the third path. He then used the uniformity model to demonstrate as clearly as possible the *group* characteristic of monopolistic competition.

It was now evident that the uniformity case had become an embarrassment. It was dangerously close to pure competition, and its diffusion assumption was inappropriate. So Chamberlin dropped the group emphasis completely. *He turned monopolistic competition instead toward the second path, ordinary monopoly—the Sraffa path.*

We must document as fully as possible the fact that Chamberlin *did* make this change, for it has sweeping consequences. It means he abandoned the greater part of the theory of monopolistic competition of chapters v to vii—the very part which textbooks had adopted as "monopolistic competition theory."

We must here recall that to Chamberlin, "monopolistic competition" was as much a set of basic ideas as it was a full-fledged theory. His conviction as to the truth of these ideas was unshaken. In this light, the necessity of rewording the theory was not catastrophic.

Yet from the standpoint of economic theory, any such change in direction is deeply important. The evidence that it was made is this: in chapter IX, the uniformity case is played down; the emphasis on groups, which had been central in earlier chapters, vanishes completely; and the stress is now on the *monopoly* characteristic of monopolistic competition, and on the significance of competition among diverse products.

Chamberlin nowhere quite says that the uniformity case has no place in monopolistic competition. His closest approach comes later, on page 301 of *General Theory of Value*, where he says that if he were doing things over, he might instead try a Marshallian "representative firm" approach. All he does in chapter IX is to insist on the uniformity case's transitional and nonrepresentative quality. It must have given him some satisfaction to be able to note that Mrs. Robinson had used a uniformity assumption throughout, whereas "in my own treatment it is an 'heroic' assumption adopted only as a temporary expedient to facilitate exposition and finally removed in order to embrace within the theory the 'diversity of conditions surrounding each producer,' which diversity is a natural concomitant of heterogeneity, with monopoly control by each producer over his own product" (p. 210).

By such references to "diversity," Chamberlin may have felt he was maintaining continuity within his work—chapters V to VII dealing principally with the uniformity case, and chapter IX with the full-fledged diversity case. But chapters V to VII were built squarely on a *group* theory of monopolistic competition. Chapter IX simply discards the group idea.

The word "group" is used only three times in chapter IX: once in connection with monopolistic competition, twice in the discussion of Mrs. Robinson's work. The group concept is not openly set aside (that comes later, in *General Theory of Value*); chapter IX only hints at its rejection. On page 198, while answering Kaldor, Chamberlin concludes that the idea of the "number of producers" (i.e., the distinction between large and small groups) lacks definite meaning in monopolistic competition. On page 201, he says that the concept of "industry" (a word he had hitherto avoided) can be seriously misleading within his theory. ("Industry" seems to be pretty much the same thing as his own "group," in this context.)

The change in direction is best illustrated by a passage on page 206, where Chamberlin says that "monopolistic competition embraces the whole theory of monopoly. But it also looks beyond, and considers the interrelations, wherever they exist, between monopolists who are in some appreciable degree of competition with each other. However great the degree of competition, it can be fully recognized by a demand curve (a) appropriately elastic, and (b) appropriately located with reference to the cost curve. It is here that the superiority of approaching the problem through the theory of monopoly rather than through that of competition is at once apparent."

So it appears that the theory of monopolistic competition, once the "heroic" assumption of uniformity is dropped, becomes the theory of ordinary monopoly. It is a theory illuminated by greater knowledge of what "ordinary monopoly" means. Chamberlin's chapter IV had established the fact that ordinary monopolists (not pure monopolists) may face the most intense competition. Nevertheless, monopolistic competition theory—at this stage in Chamberlin's thought—has become ordinary monopoly theory.

By means of this change, Chamberlin had managed to avoid the criticism that his theory was nothing but a minor variant of pure competition theory. And he had escaped the analytic tangle that results when one tries to mix the "group" idea with that of the *ceteris paribus* individual-firm demand curve. But he was now confronted with new problems.

Chamberlin was really trying to write a theory of price determination in unorganized markets (as noted at the beginning of section 4 in this essay). And *ceteris paribus* demand curves do not accurately describe the conditions facing a firm in any such market. Unorganized markets are inherently oligopolistic markets, regardless of the number of firms competitively involved. Chamberlin had not yet met Kaldor's most fundamental criticism, for chapter IX carries no indication that the monopolistic competition road is really the oligopoly road.

Moreover, Chamberlin now faced the same charge of "descriptive unrealism" which he had earlier levelled against pure competition theory. He had now written his theory—intended as a comprehensive theory of price—in monopoly terms (which means, incidentally, that he was belatedly following the path of Sraffa and Mrs. Robinson). Now if monopoly means anything, it means the possession of some genuine independence of price policy. And it simply is not true that all firms, or most firms, enjoy such independence. In real circumstances, a firm typically finds that its freedom in pricing is constrained by the presence of competitors offering close substitute products. The result is a set of prices which, even if they are not identical, are close to identity. Nobody really wants price theory which asserts that there are as many different and separate prices as there are supplying firms. Our experience of "the facts" tells us to reject the perfectly price-elastic demand curve of pure competition theory. But it tells us also to retain the idea of groups or of industries; it tells us also to retain the idea of "close substitutes," if not that of homogeneous products. And these are the ideas which Chamberlin had by now discarded.

6. THE "CHICAGO SCHOOL"

In due course, Chamberlin must have grown aware of the shortcomings of his outline of monopolistic competition theory in chapter IX; and so, in *General Theory of Value*, he turned toward oligopoly theory. But before we consider Chamberlin's final attempt, we must examine the one sustained criticism which has been directed against monopolistic competition, that made by the "Chicago School."

Chronologically, this Chicago attack falls between the 5th edition of *Monopolistic Competition* (1946) and *General Theory of Value* (1957). Considering the sweeping impact which Chamberlin's work had upon the textbooks—and the fact that revolutions in theory do not ordinarily take place without opposition—a frontal assault was surprisingly slow in appearance. The Chicago objections did not appear until the early 1950s.

There are usually considered to be three principal contributions within this Chicago broadside: Essay 2 in George Stigler's *Five Lectures on Economic Problems* (1950), Part I of Milton Friedman's *Essays in Positive Economics* (1953), and Alfred Sherrard's article in the 1951 *Journal of Political Economy*, "Advertising, Product Variation, and the Limits of Economics."

Among these three, Stigler's essay carries the most detailed criticism. In essence, its argument is this: because monopolistic competition analysis is deficient in its logical structure, it fails to provide new theory. If precise meaning is given to the somewhat nebulous concepts of "group" and "close substitutes," the result becomes very much that of pure competition. Where Chamberlin tries to draw away from pure competition, in the diversity case, his argument becomes so vague and uncertain that the analysis can hardly be ranked as theory at all. Chamberlin tells us in chapters I and IV that there is competition between diverse products, and he is right; but the theory of his later chapters tells us nothing fresh about the nature of such competition. So monopolistic competition theory leaves us no better off; and we would do better to revert to the separate theories of pure competition and monopoly, without trying to mix them.

Much or all of Stigler's criticism is valid, as we have already seen. But it leads us to the dilemma which still confronts price theory today. Economists like Sraffa, Chamberlin, and Mrs. Robinson had rebelled against the price theory of the 1920s, and their work was influential because it reflected a widespread dissatisfaction with theory which recognized only the extremes of competition and monopoly. Why then should we consider a proposal to return to this old dichotomy?

This question Milton Friedman sought to answer. The attacks on pure competition and monopoly theories, Friedman said, were based primarily on the "unrealism" of their assumptions—and this is not the way to evaluate theory. "Truly important and significant hypotheses will be found to have 'assumptions' that are wildly inaccurate descriptive representations of reality." (Friedman, p. 14) A theory must be evaluated in terms of its *predictive power*, not the "realism" of its assumptions. The theories of monopoly and pure competition are important and significant because they have predictive power.

Friedman's argument set off one of the most fascinating debates in contemporary economic literature. It rapidly became a dispute on the general question of methodology—specifically, on the place, if any, within economic analysis of those "false" or "unreal" (descriptively inaccurate) assumptions which Friedman defended. There is not much in this debate (other than in G. C. Archibald's contributions) on the matter of the relative merits of monopolistic and pure competition theories, for most of the participants were more attracted by the general methodological issue. If only on this account, we cannot here review the debate in full; all that can be done is to indicate the issues that seem most relevant to Chamberlin's work.

Friedman's argument that the only useful theory is one with predictive power has solid confirmation in physical science. This does not, however, quite vindicate his defense of "false" assumptions. A physicist may begin with a hypothesis based on certain assumptions which, according to current beliefs, are *thought to be false.* Suppose he traces the logical implications of his hypothesis and as a result finds it has predictive power: the implications conform to observed phenomena. If so, then what was *thought to be false* may not necessarily be false at all, and the results may vindicate the assumptions. In this sense, science may progress by reversing itself, by revising its beliefs in what it earlier took for granted as being "false" and "true."

Apparent falseness, then, can be defended. But Friedman seems to defend *actual* (not just apparent) falseness. The Friedman-Stigler view starts from the valid position that descriptive accuracy has no place in theory unless it has a solid analytic foundation (which the first version of monopolistic competition lacked, because of the vagueness of the "group" and "close substitutes" concepts). From this it seems to conclude that there is some actual merit in a *departure* from descriptive accuracy (falseness)—a view for which Friedman was roundly criticized in the debate which followed his essay. If a theory based on false assumptions *does* predict accurately, we have every incentive to find out why—to demonstrate that the false assumptions are really true, or else to substitute true assumptions. Short of this, the "theory" is not theory at all, for its predictive power is the power of the crystal ball.

What of the objection that most industries fall neither into the pure competition nor the monopoly category? Friedman's argument is that you can use one *or* the other. The same industry (his example is the cigarette industry) may be analyzed by using pure competition theory for one problem, and monopoly theory for another. But what happens to his "predictive power" criterion in the light of this proposal? In physical science, the predictive-power test is a test to *destroy*: a hypothesis which fails to predict must be discarded or at least amended. And it must predict *before the event*: the scientist cannot confine the predictive test to those cases which assure a successful outcome. Yet that is what Friedman seems to be proposing: as to any one industry, observe what happens, and then pick the theory, pure competition or monopoly, which happens to fit. This reduces "predictive power" to simple after-the-event rationalization.

What is the real core of the Friedman–Stigler position? Ultimately, it is an appeal for the use of price theory which is logically consistent with a view of society held ever since Adam Smith (although the Friedman–Stigler appeal is principally to Marshall)—that of a society in which virtually unlimited consumer wants press continually against a limited physical resource supply.

The nature of this ultimate appeal emerges in the third criticism of monopolistic competition mentioned earlier, that of Alfred Sherrard. Sherrard emphasizes the absolutely fundamental role of *scarcity* in economic thought. And "The problems presented by advertising and product differentiation are simply not problems of scarcity. They are therefore not manageable within the philosophical framework of economics" (p. 140).

The challenge to this philosophical framework began with Sraffa. When he brought into the open the fact of increasing returns, Sraffa was questioning the economist's view of society, whether he intended to do so or not. If production is genuinely pushing against the limits imposed by resource scarcity, then it must be production carried on under *increasing* cost conditions. These are the conditions indicated by the *rising* supply curve of pure competition—the very supply curve which Sraffa attacked.

Suppose that business firms typically operate under *de-*

creasing cost conditions, as Sraffa said they did. If output is checked by difficulties of selling more goods and not by rising production cost, if firms must engage in selling efforts to increase output, *is* there a law of scarcity?

The economist's view of society as one dominated by the fact of resource scarcity has always been challenged by Marxists, technocrats, and others. Occasionally, he has amended this view. But it has been amendment and not abandonment, for the view that there *is* a law of scarcity makes overwhelmingly more sense than any alternative hypothesis suggested.

The simplest amendment has been the monopoly amendment: one or more firms may deliberately withhold part of their possible output from the market, in order to manipulate price to their own advantage. The result is a "contrived" rather than a natural scarcity. It is to this fact which Friedman and Stigler appeal when they say we must in some instances resort to monopoly theory. And it is also, of course, the fact to which Sraffa, Mrs. Robinson, and Chamberlin appeal; in this respect we may say their differences with Friedman and Stigler are differences of detail only.

In the 1930s there emerged a more significant amendment: Keynesian economics. Keynesian theory demonstrated that the economy could settle down at an equilibrium level *below* that of full resource employment.

The bitterness with which Keynesian ideas were first opposed affords some illustration of the tenacity with which economists are prepared to defend the law of scarcity even against amendment. Today, that battle is over—and Keynesian ideas are in fact not only accepted but considered the greatest accomplishment of economics in the twentieth century.

Yet the Keynesian revolution is still incomplete. A Keynesian underemployment equilibrium presupposes *some* failure within the operating price mechanism—within the system of consumer prices, input prices, or interest rates. But Keynesian economics has not yet been extended from the macroeconomic to the microeconomic sphere, to explain just *where* within the pricing structure this failure originates. Almost certainly, it has something to do with the fact that most markets are unorganized markets. But is this failure to be explained in terms of monopoly theory? Monopoly suggests deliberate and purposeful curtailment of output; the struggles of business firms to increase their output, even if only through advertising outlays, do not seem fully consistent with a policy of output restriction.

These considerations explain the condition of price theory today: it is in a state of uneasy compromise. It is not what Chamberlin wanted, nor is it what Stigler and Friedman want. Pure competition theory is included in the textbooks because of its association with the scarcity-of-resources principle and its consequent "welfare" implications. Monopolistic competition appears, in spite of its logical weaknesses emphasized by Stigler and Friedman, because of its greater "realism" and of a continuing sense that the theories of pure competition and monopoly alone are *not* enough. The survival of Chamberlinian economics testifies to the apparent superiority of relevance over logical consistency.

7. TOWARDS A MORE GENERAL THEORY OF VALUE

Our task now is to consider Chamberlin's final attempt to work his basic ideas into the form of theory, in *General Theory of Value*. As we have seen, his position at the end of chapter IX had to be a transitional one. By outlining monopolistic competition in "ordinary monopoly" terms, he had escaped the objection that it was "too close to pure competition," and he had (apparently) avoided the problem of what his "group" meant.

But Chamberlin wanted theory applicable to the whole spectrum of competitive situations; and it is almost certainly impossible to do this in ordinary monopoly terms.

This conclusion seems confirmed by examining one further and detailed attempt at "monopoly" treatment, Robert Triffin's 1940 book, *Monopolistic Competition and General Equilibrium Theory*. This work, to a very considerable extent, took Chamberlin's chapter IX (in its original form of a *Quarterly Journal of Economics* article) as a starting point. In turn, Triffin's book had some influence on Chamberlin's ideas in *General Theory of Value*—a further reason for considering Triffin before we take up *General Theory of Value*.

Triffin himself would not have described his work as an attempt to develop "ordinary monopoly" theory. Nevertheless, Triffin most certainly wanted a theory of price in which it is *not* necessarily assumed that the firm's competitive freedom of action is limited by the fact of its membership in a homogeneous-product industry or a close-substitutes group. If a firm *does* have such independence from group ties, presumably this is because its product is "different," and in this sense its position is monopolistic.

In his increasing-returns article, Sraffa had argued for price theory constructed in *general*, not partial, equilibrium terms; now we find this argument repeated in Triffin. Marshall's partial equilibrium had meant equilibrium for an *industry*—industry being defined in homogeneous-product terms. The new emphasis on diverse product competition demanded a breaking down of the limits imposed by industries or by close-substitute groups. In Triffin we find the call for an analytic system within which it could be said of Firm A that it is in close competition with Firm B, has no perceptible competitive relation with C, and is in moderately close competition with D. Quantitative measurement is needed to replace the imprecision of "close" and "moderately close," but these terms convey the general idea.

At its outset, Triffin's book is vigorously anti-Marshallian and anti-group. The group concept, in terms of pure theory, has no significance (p. 88), it is useless (p. 89); it must be abandoned and theory built "from the concrete firm upward, without recourse to any intermediate grouping between the single firm and the whole economic collectivity" (p. 97). Yet later the tone seems to change, and we have the impression that Triffin opposes only *a priori* commitment to the group idea. He wants the group concept to prove itself empirically.

This change of emphasis indicates how difficult it is to break loose from groups. If groups, or industries, *do* exist, they dominate the behavior of their members. A firm within a homogeneous-product industry knows it must match its competitors' prices; a member of a close-substitutes group knows it must very nearly do the same thing. At least in pricing matters, this consideration so controls the environment of the firm that it has little attention to pay to outer, diverse-product competition. If groups *do* exist, a theory of price founded on the behavior of concrete firms (which is what Triffin wanted) is lost unless it starts by recognizing their existence; that is presumably why Marshall began as he did.

The analytic tool which Triffin proposed was one Kaldor had already suggested; the cross-elasticity measure. This is closely related to direct price elasticity. *Direct* elasticity measures what a change in Firm A's price will do to A's sales. *Cross* elasticity measures what this change in A's price will do to the sales *of Firm B*. And the general idea is clear: the higher this cross-elasticity value, the closer the competitive relationship between A and B.

Unfortunately, space does not permit any review here of the extensive cross-elasticity literature which followed

Triffin's work. It must be summed up by saying that the inter-firm competitive relationship cannot be summed up by any single measure, nor perhaps by any pair of measures (for as soon as Triffin got to work on cross elasticities, it became evident that at least two measures would be needed). The cross-elasticity discussion became bogged down at every point; it still has not been established to everyone's satisfaction, for example, whether the proper cross-elasticity measure between two firms in pure competition ought to be zero, infinity, or indeterminate. Moreover, some cross-elasticity articles seem to begin by assuming that groups or industries *do* exist. This brings us back to the point previously noted, that *if* they do, there is a serious question whether or not a complex device intended to measure the magnitude of diverse-product competition is really needed.

A reasonable conclusion would seem to be that the prospect of using cross elasticities to measure empirically the degree of inter-firm competition at present seems remote in the extreme. And with this, we may turn to Chamberlin's "Monopolistic Competition Revisited" essay, in *General Theory of Value*, by far the most important essay within that book.

With some simplification, this essay can be said to have two sections: an opening restatement of the basic principles, ending at the top of page 54, and a further section which seeks to give these principles new expression as theory, extending from page 54 to page 62.

With one exception, the basic principles remain as laid out in chapters I and IV of *Monopolistic Competition*. Actual competition is a blend of monopoly and competitive elements; differentiation is the key monopoly element; and the consequence of differentiation is a demand curve of less than perfect elasticity facing the seller. There is rather more emphasis on the *firm* as the essential building block in theory than there had been in *Monopolistic Competition.* This would be a minor consideration, if it did not lead into the one basic change: no emphasis on the *group.* The trend suggested in chapter IX is now confirmed; in fact, at the very close of the essay, Chamberlin says "the group has disappeared from the formulation here given."

This sounds much like the "ordinary monopoly" approach of chapter IX. But thereafter—quite suddenly, in the second section of the essay—Chamberlin turns monopolistic competition theory towards oligopoly. Thus he finally recognizes the point made in Kaldor's criticism. The original "uniformity model" had been non-oligopolistic not only because of the assumption of large numbers but also because of the vital diffusion assumption. Kaldor destroyed that model by pointing to the inappropriateness of the diffusion assumption in the types of market situations with which monopolistic competition is concerned. Without the diffusion assumption, any situation in monopolistic competition can be—and what is more, almost all situations probably are—oligopolistic, regardless of whether the number of sellers is large or small. In recognizing this, Chamberlin of course returns to the point he had made (but not followed up) in chapter V, that what appears to be a large group may in fact be an aggregation of small sub-groups.

The distinction made in the second section of Chamberlin's essay runs in these terms: it divides "isolated" from "non-isolated" sellers. (Chamberlin borrowed these two categories from Triffin's work.) The isolated seller can rely on a diffusion effect. The nonisolated seller's environment is oligopolistic; there is an awareness of mutual interdependence.

This is of course really the distinction between organized and unorganized markets once again. Suppliers on any organized commodity or security exchange are isolated sellers. They compete in a general way with other sellers, but the relation is quite impersonal. In contrast, isolated sellers are not easily found within any unorganized market.

This isolated–nonisolated distinction has not found its way into the textbooks as Chamberlin's earlier distinctions (number of sellers, differentiation or nondifferentiation of product) did, and it is easy to see why not: its appearance would disrupt much of the theory presently to be found there. The irony of the situation is that much of that theory is a consequence of Chamberlin's earlier work.

Any isolated seller firm can make its decisions on the basis of a *ceteris paribus* demand curve. It can move from one position to another upon that curve without provoking such retaliation from competitors as would change one of the "other things equal" and so change the position of the curve itself. As Chamberlin pointed out, both the pure competitor and the ordinary monopolist, supposedly so far removed from one another, are isolated sellers. To be sure, the pure competitor has an easier time sizing up his environment, for once he knows the market price he knows his demand curve, whereas the monopolist has an "information problem"—he must determine the quantitative properties of his demand curve before he can act upon it. But for many purposes, this difference between the two situations is less important than their similarity.

If a firm is an isolated seller, a theoretical description of its situation in demand curve terms is strongly indicated. But what about nonisolated sellers, those in an oligopolistic environment? Oligopoly theory has always been the weak spot in price theory. Now it transpires that almost the entire world of monopolistic competition is an oligopoly world.

It is ironic that Chamberlin, who had forced the oligopoly concept on the attention of economists, and who had finally reached an awareness of the overwhelming importance of oligopolistic interrelationships in the world he was seeking to describe, was himself unable to fashion the elements of a theory of oligopoly. Why not? Perhaps because his path was blocked by that other concept which he had popularized—product differentiation. As we have seen, he built his analysis on two elements, differentiation and fewness of sellers; these he described as "monopolistic" elements; and he had begun with a much heavier emphasis on the implications of product differentiation. He could not quite shake off his original commitment to the idea that a monopoly-like demand curve for the firm is the essential element in monopolistic competition. Yet any firm which can sum up its marketing situation in this fashion (whether it is a *ceteris paribus* demand curve or a demand curve in which the reactions of rival sellers have somehow successfully been taken account of) is not in a genuinely oligopolistic situation at all; it is an isolated seller. The essence of oligopoly is inability to separate out one's own market in this particular way.

It may have been a considerable mistake, the effects of which are still evident in the textbooks, to describe oligopoly as a particular version of monopoly; it may be that monopoly analysis has little or nothing to contribute to a theory of oligopoly. The difference between one seller and two, or one and three, or one and four, is very great indeed. If there is more than one seller, but only if there is more than one, then there is a group; and the special quality of the oligopoly problem is the resolution of group conflict. Conflict resolution, in turn, means the acceptance by group members of certain constraints upon their behavior. In such analysis, monopoly theory may perhaps have something to contribute; or it may not. (To say that the issue is simply one of "joint profit maximization" is to make a very considerable assertion regarding a problem of whose elements we know very little.)

The nature of group involvement is far more clearly evident if we think of the products of the various sellers not as differentiated but as homogeneous; it is the homogeneity of their products that binds the sellers into a group. Chamberlin of course emphasized differentiation because that was his principal escape from the theory of pure competition. Had he taken proper account of the fact that he was dealing specifically with price determination in unorganized markets, then he could have recognized that a considerable part of pure competition theory (the perfectly elastic demand curve for each firm, for example) does not necessarily apply at all in such markets—even if the products sold are homogeneous. In such markets, the terms "differentiated" and "homogeneous" require different handling, since both may be applicable at the same time. The product of unorganized-market seller A must be differentiated from that of seller B, as a matter of definition; and yet, if buyers do not consider the differentiation sufficiently important to be willing to pay a higher price for A's product than for B's, or vice versa, then the two products are also homogeneous—homogeneous, that is, with respect to the all-important matter of price.

Insofar as the preceding argument is valid, it is wrong to consider "real" competitive situations as being in some sense intermediate between monopoly and pure competition, because a critical element in these "real" situations is group involvement, an issue which is carefully skirted both in the theory of monopoly and in that of pure competition. The monopolist is assumed to be free of group membership; the firm in pure competition, through reasoning which relies implicitly on the presence of the institutions of an organized market, to have no sense of group involvement. But topics such as these move rapidly beyond the scope of the present study. Our concern is with the theory Chamberlin did write, not what he ought to have written; our interest is in the progress of his thinking, in the problems that he faced—and in the reasons why these problems arose before him.

In a sense, Chamberlin could not carry price theory any further than he did. He had pushed it close to the limit that is possible within its present methodological framework. *A priori* reasoning can tell us what an isolated seller bent on profit maximization will do; and so theory leans toward isolated-seller analysis; it tells us profit maximization means the equation of marginal revenue and marginal cost. But *a priori* reasoning canot tell us how supplying firms will behave in an oligopolistic environment. So far as deduction goes, the outcome is "indeterminate." Things are not really indeterminate, of course, for in practice an outcome is established—and in all probability there exists within oligopoly situations a uniformity of behavior patterns which it is the task of theory to uncover and describe. But deductive analysis has reached its limit at this stage, until fresh "evidence" is brought in—that is, until more empirical work is done to establish the behavior that is typical in an environment of mutual interdependence. Until this is done, price theory is unlikely to advance much beyond its present stage.

Chamberlin's instincts were sound when he tried to begin with a theory which recognized groups and yet involved something less than the perfectly elastic demand curve of pure competition. His mistake was the mistake of many others, to think that the road away from pure competition's results had to be the road toward monopoly. And here we may recall that in chapter v of *Monopolistic Competition*, Chamberlin noted (but did not follow up) the fact that firms may tacitly agree to accept a given price. He was in effect saying that firms may try to avoid the uncertainty of an oligopolistic environment by mutual acceptance of that price; and the acceptance of this behavior constraint means giving up whatever "monopoly" control over price which each firm might otherwise have possessed. Had ideas such as this been followed up earlier, monopolistic competition theory would have developed quite differently.

Hence we reach once again the conclusion indicated early in this study, that price analysis—like many other areas of human inquiry—is so appallingly complex that any success in theory is at best partial success. Ultimately, Chamberlin was defeated as Marshall was defeated, because he could not incorporate within formal theory all of his ideas and all of his insights. Nevertheless, Chamberlin's work altered every aspect of price analysis which it touched. The theory of pure competition was never quite the same after Chamberlin's assault. At the other competitive extreme, Chamberlin threw new light on the theory of monopoly—even his Chicago critics conceded this. And although he did not establish the theory of oligopoly which his objective demanded, Chamberlin almost single-handedly introduced the concept of oligopoly and forced it on the attention of economists. So the evaluation of *Monopolistic Competition* quoted in the first paragraph of this study still stands: "the most influential single work ever produced by an American economist."

BIBLIOGRAPHY

Andrews, P. W. S. *On Competition In Economic Theory*. London, Macmillan, 1964.

Archibald, G. C. "Chamberlin *versus* Chicago," *Review of Economic Studies*, XXIX (October 1961), 2–21.

Bain, Joe S. *et al.* "The Theory of Monopolistic Competition After Thirty Years," *American Economic Review, Papers and Proceedings,* LIV (May 1964), 28–57.

Bishop, Robert L. "Elasticities, Cross-Elasticities, and Market Relationships," *American Economic Review,* XLII (December 1952), 779–803.

Chamberlin, Edward H. *The Theory of Monopolistic Competition.* Cambridge, Harvard University Press, 1st ed., 1933; 5th ed., 1946; 8th ed., 1962.

—— *Towards a More General Theory of Value.* New York, Oxford University Press, 1957.

—— "The Origin and Early Development of Monopolistic Competition Theory," *Quarterly Journal of Economics,* LXXV (November 1961), 515–43.

Clapham, J. H. "Of Empty Economic Boxes," *Economic Journal,* XXXII (1922), 305–14. Reprinted in George J. Stigler and Kenneth E. Boulding, eds., *Readings in Price Theory.* Chicago, Irwin, 1952.

Demsetz, Harold. "The Nature of Equilibrium in Monopolistic Competition," *Journal of Political Economy,* LXVII (February 1959), 21–30.

Dewey, Donald. "Imperfect Competition No Bar to Efficient Production," *Journal of Political Economy,* LXVI (February 1958), 24–33.

Friedman, Milton. *Essays in Positive Economics.* Chicago, University of Chicago Press, 1953. See especially Part I, "The Methodology of Positive Economics."

Frisch, Ragnar. "Alfred Marshall's Theory of Value," *Quarterly Journal of Economics,* LXIV (November 1950), 495–524.

Hague, D. C. "Alfred Marshall and the Competitive Firm," *Economic Journal,* LXVIII (December 1959), 673–90.

Kaldor, Nicholas. "Market Imperfection and Excess Capacity," *Economica,* New Series II (February 1935), pp. 33–50. Reprinted in George J. Stigler and Kenneth E. Boulding, eds., *Readings in Price Theory.* Chicago, Irwin, 1952.

—— "Mrs. Robinson's 'Economics of Imperfect Competition,'" *Economica,* New Series I (August 1934), 335–41.

—— "Professor Chamberlin on Monopolistic and Imperfect Competition," *Quarterly Journal of Economics*, LII (May 1938), 513–38.

Kuenne, Robert E., ed. *Monopolistic Competition Theory: Studies in Impact*. New York, Wiley, 1967.

Machlup, Fritz. "Professor Samuelson on Theory and Realism," and Samuelson, "Theory and Realism: A Reply," *American Economic Review*, LIV (September 1964), 733–39.

Marshall, Alfred. *Industry and Trade*. 4th ed. London: Macmillan, 1923.

—— *Principles of Economics*. 8th ed. London, Macmillan, 1947.

Massey, Gerald J. "Professor Samuelson on Theory and Realism: Comment," and Samuelson, "Reply," *American Economic Review*, LV (December 1965), 1155–72.

Maxwell, J. A. "Some Marshallian Concepts, Especially the Representative Firm," *Economic Journal*, LXVIII (December 1959), 691–98.

Newman, Peter. "The Erosion of Marshall's Theory of Value," *Quarterly Journal of Economics*, LXXIV (November 1960), 587–600.

Papandreou, A. G. "Market Structure and Monopoly Power," *American Economic Review*, XXXIX (September 1949), 883–97.

Pigou, A. C., ed. *Memorials of Alfred Marshall*. London, Macmillan, 1925.

Robinson, Joan. *The Economics of Imperfect Competition*. London, Macmillan, 1933.

Samuelson, Paul A. "Problems of Methodology: Discussion," *American Economic Review, Papers & Proceedings*, LIII (May 1963), 231–36.

Schumpeter, Joseph. *History of Economic Analysis*, New York, Oxford University Press, 1954.

Sherrard, Alfred. "Advertising, Product Variation, and the Limits of Economics," *Journal of Political Economy*, LIX (April 1951), 126–42.

Sraffa, Piero. "The Laws of Return Under Competitive Conditions," *Economic Journal*, XXXVI (1926), 535–50. Reprinted in George Stigler and Kenneth E. Boulding, eds., *Readings in Price Theory*. Chicago, Irwin, 1952.

Stigler, George. *Five Lectures on Economic Problems*. London,

Macmillan, 1950. See especially Lecture 2, "Monopolistic Competition in Retrospect."

Triffin, Robert. *Monopolistic Competition and General Equilibrium Theory*. Cambridge, Harvard University Press, 1940.

Wolfe, J. N. "The Representative Firm," *Economic Journal*, LXIV (June 1954), 337–49.